Buddha or Karl Marx

By

Dr. B. R. Ambedkar

Published By

Charlies Technology, India

ISBN-13: 978-1517205218

ISBN-10: 1517205212

Contents

I. THE CREED OF THE BUDDHA
II. THE ORIGINAL CREED OF KARL MARX
III. WHAT SURVIVES OF THE MARXIAN CREED
IV. COMPARISON BETWEEN BUDDHA AND KARL MARX
V. **THE MEANS**
VI. **EVALUATION OF MEANS**
VII. WHOSE MEANS ARE MORE EFFICACIOUS
VIII. WITHERING AWAY OF THE STATE

Editorial Note in the source publication: Dr. Babasaheb Ambedkar: Writings and Speeches, Vol. 3:

The Committee found three different typed copies of an essay on Buddha and Karl Marx in loose sheets, two of which have corrections in the author's own handwriting. After scrutinising these, this essay is compiled incorporating the corrections. The essay is divided into sub-topics as shown below: Introduction
  1. *The Creed of the Buddha*
  2. *The Original Creed of Karl Marx*
  3. *What survives of the Marxian Creed?*
  4. *Comparison between Buddha and Karl Marx*
  5. *Means*
  6. *Evaluation of Means*
  7. *Whose Means are More Efficacious?*
  8. *Withering away of the State*
  — *Editors.*

A comparison between Karl Marx and Buddha may be regarded as a joke. There need be no surprise in this. Marx and Buddha are divided by 2381 years. Buddha was born in 563 BC and Karl Marx in 1818 AD Karl Marx is supposed to be the architect of a new ideology-polity a new Economic system. The Buddha on the other hand is believed to be no more than the founder of a religion, which has no relation to politics or economics. The heading of this essay " Buddha or Karl Marx " which suggests either a comparison or a contrast between two such personalities divided by such a lengthy span of time and occupied with different fields of thought is sure to sound odd. The Marxists may easily laugh at it and may ridicule the very idea of treating Marx and Buddha on the same level. Marx so modern and Buddha so ancient! The Marxists may say that the Buddha as compared to their master must be just primitive. What comparison can there be between two such persons? What could a Marxist learn from the Buddha? What can Buddha teach a Marxist? None-the-less a comparison between the two is a attractive and instructive Having read both and being interested in the ideology of both a comparison between them just forces itself on me. If the Marxists keep back their prejudices and study the Buddha and understand what he stood for I feel sure that they will change their attitude. It is of course too much to expect that having been determined to scoff at the Buddha they will remain to pray. But this much can he said that they will realise that there is something in the Buddha's teachings which is worth their while to take note of.

I THE CREED OF THE BUDDHA

The Buddha is generally associated with the doctrine of Ahimsa. That is taken to be the be-all and end-all of his teachings. Hardly anyone knows that what the Buddha taught is something very vast: far beyond Ahimsa. It is therefore necessary to set out in detail his tenets. I enumerate them below as I have understood them from my reading of the Tripitaka :
1. Religion is necessary for a free Society.
2. Not every Religion is worth having. 3. Religion must relate to facts of life and not to theories and speculations about God, or Soul or Heaven *or* Earth.
4. It is wrong to make God the centre of Religion.

5. It is wrong to make salvation of the soul as the centre of Religion.

6. It is wrong to make animal sacrifices to be the centre of religion.

7. Real Religion lives in the heart of man and not in the Shastras.

8. Man and morality must be the centre of religion. If not, Religion is a cruel superstition.

9. It is not enough for Morality to be the ideal of life. Since there is no God it must become the Jaw of life. 10. The function of Religion is to reconstruct the world and to make it happy and not to explain its origin or its end.

11. That the unhappiness in the world is due to conflict of interest and the only way to solve it is to follow the Ashtanga Marga.

12. That private ownership of property brings power to one class and sorrow to another.

13. That it is necessary for the good of Society that this sorrow be removed by removing its cause.

14. All human beings are equal.

15. Worth and not birth is the measure of man.

16. What is important is high ideals and not noble birth.

17. Maitri or fellowship towards all must never be abandoned. One owes it even to one's enemy.

18. Every one has a right to learn. Learning is as necessary for man to live as food is.

19. Learning without character is dangerous.

20. Nothing is infallible. Nothing is binding forever. Every thing is subject to inquiry and examination. 21. Nothing is final.

22. Every thing is subject to the law of causation.

23. Nothing is permanent or sanatan. Every thing is subject to change. Being is always becoming.

24. War is wrong unless it is for truth and justice.

25. The victor has duties towards the vanquished. This is the creed of the Buddha in a summary form. How ancient hut how fresh! How wide and how deep are his teachings!

II THE ORIGINAL CREED OF KARL MARX

Let us now turn to the creed of Karl Marx as originally propounded by him. Karl Marx is no doubt the father of modern socialism or Communism but he was not interested merely in propounding the theory of Socialism. That had been done long before him by others. Marx was more interested in proving that his Socialism was scientific. His crusade was as much against the capitalists as it was against those whom he called the Utopian Socialists. He disliked them both. It is necessary to note this point because Marx attached the greatest importance to the scientific character of his Socialism. All the doctrines which Marx propounded had no other purpose than to establish his contention that his brand of Socialism was scientific and not Utopian.

By scientific socialism what Karl Marx meant was that his brand of socialism was *inevitable* and *inescapable* and that society was moving towards it and that nothing could prevent its march. It is to prove this contention of his that Marx principally laboured. Marx's contention rested on the following theses. They were:—

(i) That the purpose of philosophy is to reconstruct the world and not to explain the origin of the universe.

(ii) That the force which shapes the course of history are primarily economic.

(iii) That society is divided into two classes, owners and workers. (iv) That there is always a class conflict going on between the two classes.

(v) That the workers are exploited by the owners who misappropriate the surplus value, which is the result of the workers' labour.

(vi) That this exploitation can be put an end to by nationalisation of the instruments of production i.e. abolition of private property.

(vii) That this exploitation is leading to greater and greater impoverishment of the workers.

(viii) That this growing impoverishment of the workers is resulting in a revolutionary spirit among the workers *and* the conversion of the class conflict into a class struggle.

(ix) That as the workers outnumber the owners, the workers are bound to capture the State and establish their rule, which he called the dictatorship of the proletariat.

(x) These factors are irresistible and therefore socialism is inevitable.

I hope I have reported correctly the propositions, which formed the original basis of Marxian Socialism.

III WHAT SURVIVES OF THE MARXIAN CREED

Before making a comparison between the ideologies of the Buddha and Karl Marx it is necessary to note how much of this original corpus of the Marxian creed has survived; how much has been disproved by history and how much has been demolished by his opponents.

The Marxian Creed was propounded sometime in the middle of the nineteenth century. Since then it has been subjected to much criticism. As a result of this criticism much of the ideological structure raised by Karl Marx has broken to pieces. There is hardly any doubt that Marxist claim that his socialism was inevitable has been completely disproved. The dictatorship of the Proletariat was first established in 1917 in one country after a period of something like seventy years after the publication of his *Das Capital* the gospel of socialism. Even when the Communism—which is another name for the dictatorship of the Proletariat—came to Russia, it did not come as something inevitable without any kind of human effort. There was a revolution and much deliberate planning had to be done with a lot of violence and blood shed, before it could step into Russia. The rest of the world is still waiting for coming of the Proletarian Dictatorship. Apart from this general falsification of the Marxian thesis that Socialism is inevitable, many of the other propositions stated in the lists have also been demolished both by logic as well as by experience. Nobody now I accepts the economic interpretation of history as the only explanation of history. Nobody accepts that the proletariat has been progressively pauperised. And the same is true about his other premises.

What remains of the Karl Marx is a residue of fire, small but still very important. The residue in my view consists of four items:

(i) The function of philosophy is to reconstruct the world and not to waste its time in explaining the origin of the world. (ii) That there is a conflict of interest between class and class. (iii) That private ownership of property brings power to one class and sorrow to another through exploitation.

(iv) That it is necessary for the good of society that the sorrow be removed by the abolition of private property.

IV COMPARISON BETWEEN BUDDHA AND KARL MARX

Taking the points from the Marxian Creed which have survived one may now enter upon a comparison between the Buddha and Karl Marx.

On the first point there is complete agreement between the Buddha and Karl Marx. To show how close is the agreement I quote below a part of the dialogue between Buddha and the Brahmin Potthapada.

"Then, in the same terms, Potthapada asked (the Buddha) each of the following questions:

1. Is the world not eternal?
2. Is the world finite?
3. Is the world infinite?
4. Is the soul the same as the body?
5. Is the soul one thing, and the body another?
6. Does one who has gained the truth live again after death ?
7. Does he neither live again, nor not live again, after death ? And to each question the exalted one made the same reply: It was this.

"That too, Potthapada, is a matter on which I have expressed no opinion ".

28. " But why has the Exalted One expressed no opinion on that ? " (Because) 'This question is not calculated to profit, it is not concerned with (the Dhamma) it does not redound even to the elements of right conduct, nor to detachment nor to purification from lust, nor to quietude, nor to tranquillisation of heart, nor to real knowledge, nor to the insight (of the higher stages of the Path), nor to Nirvana. Therefore it is that I express no opinion upon it. " On the second point I give below

a quotation from a dialogue between Buddha and Pasenadi King of Kosala:

" Moreover, there is always strife going on between kings, between ' nobles, between Brahmins, between house holders, between mother and son, between son and father, between brother and sister, , between sister and brother, between companion and companion. . ." ' Although these are the words of Pasenadi, the Buddha did not deny that they formed a true picture of society.

As to the Buddha's own attitude towards class conflict his doctrine ". of Ashtanga Marga recognises that class conflict exists and that it is ; the class conflict which is the cause of misery.

On the third question I quote from the same dialogue of Buddha with Potthapada;

" Then what is it that the Exalted One has determined?
" " I have expounded, Potthapada, that sorrow and misery exist! " I have expounded, what is the origin of misery. I have expounded what is the cessation of misery: I have expounded what is method by which one may reach the cessation of misery.

30. 'And why has the Exalted One put forth a statement as to that?'

' Because that questions Potthapada, is calculated to profit, is concerned with the Dhamma redounds to the beginnings of right conduct, to detachment, to purification from lusts, to quietude, to tranquillisation of heart, to real knowledge, to the insight of the higher stages of the Path and to Nirvana. Therefore is it, Potthapada that I have put forward a statement as to that. '

That language is different but the meaning is the same. If for misery one reads exploitation Buddha is not away from Marx.

On the question of private property the following extract from a dialogue between Buddha and Ananda is very illuminating. In reply to a question by Ananda the Buddha said:

"I have said that avarice is because of possession. Now in what way that is so, Ananda, is to be understood after this manner. Where there is no possession of any sort or kind whatever by any one or anything, then there being no possession whatever, would there, owing to this cessation of possession, be any appearance of avarice? " 'There would not. Lord".

'Wherefore, Ananda, just that is the ground, the basis, the genesis, the cause of avarice, to wit, possession.

31. 'I have said that tenacity is the cause possession. Now in what way that is so, Ananda, is to be understood after this manner. Were there no tenacity of any sort or kind whatever shown by any one with respect to any thing, then there being whatever, would there owing to this cessation of tenacity, be any appearance of possession? ' 'There would not. Lord.'

'Wherefore, Ananda, just that is the ground, the basis, the genesis, the cause of possession, to wit tenacity. '
On the fourth point no evidence is necessary. The rules of the Bhikshu Sangh will serve as the best testimony on the subject.

According to the rules a Bhikku can have private property only in the following eight articles and no more. These eight articles are: —

1. |
2. } Three robes or pieces of cloth for daily wear.
3. |
4. A girdle for the loins.
5. An alms-bowl.
6. A razor.
7. A needle.
8. A water strainer.

Further a Bhikku was completely forbidden to receive gold or silver for fear that with gold or silver he might buy some thing beside the eight things he is permitted to have.

These rules are far more rigorous than are to be found in communism in Russia.

V THE MEANS

We must now come to the means. The means of bringing about Communism, which the Buddha propounded, were quite definite. The means can he decided into three parts. Part I consisted in observing the Pancha Silas. The Enlightenment gave birth to a new gospel, which contains the key to the solution *of* the problem, which was haunting him.

The foundation of the New Gospel is the fact that the world was full of misery and unhappiness. It was fact not merely to be noted but to be regarded as being the first and foremost in any scheme of salvation. The recognition of this fact the Buddha made the starting point of his gospel.

To remove this misery and unhappiness was to him the aim and object of the gospel if it is to serve any useful purpose.

Asking what could be the causes of this misery the Buddha found that there could be only two.

A part of the misery and unhappiness of man was the result of his own misconduct. To remove this cause of misery he preached the practice of Panch Sila.

The Panch Sila comprised the following observations: (1) To abstain from destroying or causing destruction of any living things (2) To abstain from stealing i.e. acquiring or keeping by fraud or violence, the property of another: (3) To Abstain from telling untruth: (4) To abstain from lust: (5) To abstain from intoxicating drinks.

A part of the misery and unhappiness in the world was according to the Buddha the result of man's inequity towards man. How was this inequity to be removed ? For the removal of man's inequity towards man the Buddha prescribed the Noble Eight-Fold Path. The elements of the Noble Fight-Fold Path are:

(1) Right views i.e. freedom from superstition: (2) Right aims, high and worthy of the intelligent and earnest men; (3) Right speech i.e. kindly, open, truthful: (4) Right Conduct i.e. peaceful, honest and pure; (5) Right livelihood i.e. causing hurt or injury to no living being; (6) Right perseverance in all the other seven; (7) Right mindfulness i.e. with a watchful and active mind; and (8) Right contemplation i.e. earnest thought on the deep mysteries of life.

The aim of the Noble Eight-Fold Path is to establish on earth the kingdom of righteousness, and thereby to banish sorrow and unhappiness from the face of the world.

The third part of the Gospel is the doctrine of Nibbana. The doctrine of Nibbana is an integral part of the doctrine of the Noble Eight-Fold Path. Without Nibbana the realisation of the Eight-Fold Path cannot be accomplished.

The doctrine of Nibbana tells what are the difficulties in the way of the realisation of the Eight-Fold Path.

The chiefs of these difficulties are ten in number. The Buddha called them the Ten Asavas, Fetters or Hindrances.

The first hindrance is the delusion of self. So long as a man is wholly occupied with himself, chasing after every bauble that he vainly thinks will satisfy the cravings of his heart, there is no noble path for him. Only when his eyes have been opened to the fact that he is but a tiny part of a measureless, whole, only when he begins to realise how impermanent a thing is his temporary individuality can he even enter upon this narrow path.

The second is Doubt and Indecision. When a man's eyes are opened to the great mystery of existence, the impermanence of every individuality, he is likely to be assailed by doubt and indecision as to his action. To do or not to do, after all my individuality is impermanent, why do anything are questions, which make him indecisive or inactive. But that will not do in life. He must make up his mind to follow the teacher, to accept the truth and to enter on the struggle or he will get no further.

The third is dependence on the efficacy of Rites and Ceremonies. No good resolutions, however firm will lead *to* anything unless a man gets rid of ritualism: of the belief that any outward acts. any priestly powers, and holy ceremonies, can afford him an assistance of any kind. It is only when he has overcome this hindrance, that men can be said to have fairly entered upon the stream and has a chance sooner or later to win a victory.

" The fourth consists of the bodily passions... The fifth is ill will towards other individuals. The sixth is the suppression of the desire for a future life with a material body and the seventh is the desire for a future life in an immaterial world.

The eighth hindrance is Pride and nineth is self-righteousness. These are failings which it is most difficult for men to overcome, and to which superior minds are peculiarly liable a Praisaical contempt for those who are less able and less holy than themselves.

The tenth hindrance is ignorance. When all other difficulties are conquered this will even remain, the thorn in the flesh of the wise a.nd good, the last enemy and the bitterest foe of man.

Nibbana consists in overcoming these hindrances to the pursuit of the Noble Eight-Fold Path.

The doctrine of the Noble Eight-Fold Path tells what disposition of the mind which a person should sedulously cultivate. The doctrine of Nibbana tells of the temptation or hindrance which a person should earnestly overcome if he wishes to trade along with the Noble Eight-Fold Path

The Fourth Part of the new Gospel is the doctrine of Paramitas. The doctrine of Paraimitas inculcates the practice of ten virtues in one's daily life.

These are those ten virtues—d) Panna (2) Sila (3) Nekkhama (4) Dana(5) Virya(6) Khanti(7) Succa(8) Aditthana(9) Mettaa-nd (10) Upekkha.

Panna or wisdom is the light that removes the darkenss of Avijja, Moha or Nescience. The Panna requires that one must get all his doubts removed by questioning those wiser than him self, associate with the wise and cultivate the different arts and sciences which help to develop the mind.

Sila is moral temperament, the disposition not to do evil and the disposition to do good; to be ashamed of doing wrong. To avoid doing evil for fear of punishment is Sila. Sila means fear of doing wrong. Nekkhama is renunciation of the pleasures of the world. Dana means the giving of one's possessions, blood and limbs and even one's life for the good of the others without expecting anything in return.

Virya is right endeavour. It is doing with all your might with thought never turning back, whatever you have undertaken to do.

Khanti is forbearance. Not to meet hatred by harted is the essence of it. For hatred is not appeased by hatred. It is appeased only by forbearance.

Succa is truth. An aspirant for Buddha never speaks a lie. His speech is truth and nothing but truth.

Aditthana is resolute determination to reach the goal. Metta is fellow feeling extending to all beings, foe and friend, beast and man.

Upekka is detachment as distinguished from indifference. It is a state of mind where there is neither like nor dislike. Remaining unmoved by the result and yet engaged in the pursuit of it.

These virtues one must practice to his utmost capacity. That is why they are called Paramitas (States of Perfection).

Such is the gospel the Buddha enunciated as a result of his enlightenment to end the sorrow and misery in the world.

It is clear that the means adopted by the Buddha were to convert a man by changing his moral disposition to follow the path voluntarily.

The means adopted by the Communists are equally clear, short and swift. They are (1) Violence and (2) Dictatorship *of* the Proletariat.

The Communists say that there are the only two means of establishing communism. The first is violence. Nothing short of it will suffice to break up the existing system. The other is dictatorship of the proletariat. Nothing short of it will suffice to continue the new system.

It is now clear what are the similarities and differences between Buddha and Karl Marx. The differences are about the means. The end is common to both.

VI EVALUATION OF MEANS

We must now turn to the evaluation of means. We must ask whose means are superior and lasting in the long run. There are, however some misunderstandings on both sides. It is necessary to clear them up. Take violence. As to violence there are many people who seem to shiver at the very thought of it. But this is only a sentiment. Violence cannot be altogether dispensed with. Even in non-communist countries a murderer is hanged. Does not hanging amount to violence? Non-communist countries go to war with non-communist countries. Millions of people are killed. Is this no violence? If a murderer can be killed, because he has killed a citizen, if a soldier can be killed in war because he belongs to a hostile nation why cannot a property owner be killed if his ownership leads to misery for the rest of humanity? There is no reason to make an exception in favour of the property owner, why one should regard private property as sacrosanct.

The Buddha was against violence. But he was also in favour of justice and where justice required he permitted the use of force. This is well illustrated in his dialogue with Sinha Senapati the Commander-in-Chief of Vaishali. Sinha having come to know that the Buddha preached Ahimsa went to him and asked:

"The Bhagvan preaches Ahimsa. Does the Bhagvan preach an offender to be given freedom from punishment? Does the Bhagvan preach that we should not go to war to save our wives, our children and our wealth? Should we suffer at the hands of criminals in the name of Ahimsa.?"

" Does the Tathagata prohibit all war even when it is in the interest of Truth and Justice?"

Buddha replied. You have wrongly understood what I have been preaching. An offender must be punished and an innocent man must be freed. It is not a fault of the Magistrate if he punishes an offender. The cause of punishment is the fault of the offender. The Magistrate who inflicts the punishment is only carrying out the law. He does not become stained with Ahimsa. A man who fights for justice and safety cannot be accused of Ahimsa. If all the means of maintaining peace have failed then the responsibility for Himsa falls on him who starts war. One must never surrender to evil powers. War there may be. But it must not be for selfish ends...."

There are of course other grounds against violence such as those urged by Prof. John Dewey. In dealing with those who contend that the end justifies the means is morally perverted doctrine, Dewey has rightly asked what can justify the means if not the end ? It is only the end that can justify the means.

Buddha would have probably admitted that it is only the end which would justify the means. What else could? And he would have said that if the end justified violence, violence was a legitimate means for the end in view. He certainly would not have exempted property owners from force if force were the only means for that end. As we shall see his means for the end were different. As Prof. Dewey has pointed out that violence is only another name for the use of force and although force must be used for creative purposes a distinction between use of force as energy and use of force as violence needs to be made. The achievement of an end involves the destruction of many other ends, which are integral with the one that is sought to be destroyed. Use of force must be so regulated that it should save as many ends as possible in destroying the evil one. Buddha's Ahimsa was not as absolute as the Ahimsa preached by Mahavira the founder of Jainism. He would have allowed force only as energy. The communists preach Ahimsa as an absolute principle. To this the Buddha was deadly opposed.

As to Dictatorship the Buddha would have none of it. He was born a democrat and he died a democrat. At the time he lived there were 14 monarchical states and 4 republics. He belonged to the Sakyas and the Sakya's kingdom was a republic. He was extremely in love with Vaishali which was his second home because it was a republic. Before his Mahaparinirbban he spent his Varshavasa in Vaishali. After the completion of his Varshavasa he decided to leave Vaishali and go elsewhere as was his wont. After going some distance he looked back on Vaishali and said to Ananda. "This is the last look of Vaishali which the Tathagata is having ". So fond was he of this republic.

He was a thorough equalitarian. Originally the Bhikkus, including the Buddha himself, wore robes made of rags. This rule was enunciated to prevent the aristocratic classes from joining the Sangh. Later Jeevaka the great physician prevailed upon the Buddha to accept a robe, which was made of a whole cloth. The Buddha at once altered the rule and extended it to all the monks.

Once the Buddha's mother Mahaprajapati Gotami who had joined the Bhikkuni Sangh heard that the Buddha had got a chill. She at once started preparing a scarf for him. After having completed it she took to the Buddha and asked him to wear it. But he refused to accept it saying that if it is a gift it must be a gift to the whole Sangh and not to an individual member of the Sangh. She pleaded and pleaded but he refused to yield.

The Bhikshu Sangh had the most democratic constitution. He was only one of the Bhikkus. At the most he was like a Prime Minister among members of the Cabinet. He was never a dictator. Twice before his death he was asked to appoint some one as the head of the Sangh to control it. But each time he refused saying that the Dhamma is the Supreme

Commander of the Sangh. He refused to be a dictator and refused to appoint a dictator.

What about the value of the means? Whose means are superior and lasting in the long run?

Can the Communists say that in achieving their valuable end they have not destroyed other valuable ends? They have destroyed private property. Assuming that this is a valuable end can the Communists say that they have not destroyed other valuable end in the process of achieving it? How many people have they killed for achieving their end. Has human life no value? Could they not have taken property without taking the life of the owner?

Take dictatorship. The end of Dictatorship is to make the Revolution a permanent revolution. This is a valuable end. But can the Communists say that in achieving this end they have not destroyed other valuable ends? Dictatorship is often defined as absence of liberty or absence of Parliamentary Government. Both interpretations are not quite clear. There is no liberty even when there is Parliamentary Government. For law means want of liberty. The difference between Dictatorship and Parliamentary Govt. lies in this. In Parliamentary Government every citizen has a right to criticise the restraint on liberty imposed by the Government. In Parliamentary Government you have a duty and a right; the duty to obey the law and right to criticise it. In Dictatorship you have only duty to obey but no right to criticise it.

VII WHOSE MEANS ARE MORE EFFICACIOUS

We must now consider whose means are more lasting. One has to choose between Government by force and Government by moral disposition.

As Burke has said force cannot be a lasting means. In his speech on conciliation with America he uttered this memorable warning:

" First, Sir, permit me to observe, that the use of force alone is but temporary. It may subdue for a moment; but it does not remove the necessity of subduing again; and a nation is not governed which is perpetually to be conquered. "

" My next objection is its uncertainty. Terror is not always the effect of force, and an armament is not a victory. If you do not succeed, you are without resource, for, conciliation failing, force remains; but force failing, no further hope of reconciliation is left. Power and authority are sometimes bought by kindness; but they can never be begged as alms by an impoverished and defeated violence.

A further objection to force is that you impair the object by your very endeavours to preserve it. The thing you fought for is the thing, which you recover, but depreciated, sunk, wasted and consumed in the contest. "

In a sermon addressed to the Bhikkus the Buddha has shown the difference between the rule by Righteousness and Rule by law i.e. force. Addressing the Brethren he said:

(2) Long ago, brethren, there was Sovereign overlord named Strongtyre, a king ruling in righteousness, lord of the four quarters of the earth, conqueror, the protector of his people. He was the possessor of the celestial wheel. He lived in supremacy over this earth to its ocean bounds, having conquered it, not by the courage, by the sword, but by righteousness.

(3) Now, brethren, after many years, after many hundred years. after manu thousand years, king Strongtyre command a certain man, saying:

"Thou should est see, Sir, the Celestial Wheel has sunk a little, has slipped down from its place, bring me word. "

Now after many many hundred years had slipped down from its place On seeing this he went to King Strongtyre and said: "Know. sir, for a truth that the Celestial Wheel has sunk, has slipped down from its place. "

The king Strongtyre, brethren, let the prince his eldest son be sent for and speak thus:

' Behold, dear boy, my Celestial Wheel has sunk a little, has slipped down from its place. Now it has been told me; If the Celestial Wheel of a wheel turning King shall sink down, shall slip down from its place, that king has not much longer to live. I have had my fill of human pleasures; 'It's time to seek after divine joys, Come, dear boy, take thou charge over this earth bounded by the ocean. But I, shaving, hair and beard, and donning yellow robes, will go forth from home into the homeless state.

So brethren. King Strongtyre, having in due form established his eldest son on the throne, shaved hair and bearded, donned yellow robes and went forth from home into homeless state. But on the seventh day after the royal hermit had gone forth, the Celestial Wheel disappeared.

(4) Then a certain man went to the King, and told him, saying: Know, 0 King, for a truth, that the Celestial Wheel has disappeared!

Then that King, brethren, was grieved thereat and afflicted with sorrow. And he went to the royal hermit, and told him, saying, Know, sir, for a truth, that the Celestial Wheel has disappeared.

And the anointed king so saying, the royal hermit made reply. Grieve thou not, dear son, that the Celestial Wheel has disappeared, nor be afflicted that the Celestial Wheel has disappeared. For no paternal heritage of thin, dear son, is the Celestial Wheel. But verily, dear son, turn thou in the Ariyan turning of the Wheel-turners. (Act up to the noble ideal of duty set before themselves by the true sovereigns of the world). Then it may well be that if thou carry out the Ariyan duty of a Wheel-turning Monarch, and on the feast of the moon thou wilt for, with bathed head to keep the feast on the chief upper terrace, to the Celestial Wheel will manifest, itself with its thousand spokes its tyre, navel and all its part complete. (5) 'Put what, sire is this Ariya duty of a Wheel-turning Monarch?' This, dear son, that thou, leaning on the Norm (the law of truth and righteousness) honouring, respecting and revering it, doing homage to it, hallowing it, being thyself a Norm-banner, a Norm-signal, having the Norm as thy master, should provide the right watch, ward, and protection for thine own folk, for the army, for the nobles, for vassals, for brahmins and house holders, for town and country dwellers, for the religious world, and for beasts and birds. Throughout thy kingdom let no wrongdoing prevail. And whosoever in thy kingdom is poor, to him let wealth be given.

' And when dear son, in thy kingdom men of religious life, renouncing the carelessness arising from intoxication of the senses, and devoted to forbearance and sympathy, each mastering self, each claiming self, each protecting self, shall come to thee from time to time, and question the concerning what is good and what is bad. what is criminal and what is not, what is to be done and what is to be left undone, what line of action will in the long run work for weal or for woe, thou shouldest hear what they have to say and thou shouldest deter them from evil, and bid them take up what is good. This, dear son, is the Ariyan duty of a sovereign of the world.'

' Even so, ' sire, answered the anointed king, and obeying, and carried out the Ariyan duty of a sovereign lord. To him, thus behaving, when on the feast of the full moon he had gone in the observance with bathed head to the chief upper Terrance the Celestial Wheel revealed itself, with its thousand spokes, its tyre. its naval, and all its part complete. And seeing this is occurred to the king: ' It has been told me that a king to whom on such a occasion the Celestial Wheel reveals itself completely, becomes a Wheel-turning monarch. May I even I also become a sovereign of the world.'

(6) Then brethren, the king arose from his seat and uncovering his robe from one shoulder, took in his left hand a pitcher, and with his right hand sprinkled up over the Celestial Wheel, saying: ' Roll onward, O Lord Wheel! Go forth and overcome, O Lord Wheel ! ' Then, brethren, the Celestial Wheel rolled onwards towards the region of the East. and after it went the Wheel-turning king, and with him his army, horses and chariots and elephants and men. And in whatever place, brethren, the wheel stopped, there the king, the victorious warlord, took up his abode, and with him his fourfold army. Then the all, the rival kings in the region of the East came to the sovereign king and said 'Come, O mighty king! Welcome, O mighty king! All is thine, O mighty King! Teach us, O mighty king! '

The king, the sovereign war-lord, speak thus: 'Ye shall slay no living thing. Ye shall not take that which has not been given. Ye shall not act wrongly touching bodily desires. Ye shall speak no lie. Ye shall drink no maddening drink. Enjoy your possessions as you have been wont to do.'

(7) Then, brethren, the Celestial Wheel, plunging down to the Eastern ocean, rose up out again, and rolled onwards to

the region of the south.... (and there all happened as had happened in the East). And in like manner the Celestial Wheel, plunging into Southern ocean, rose up out again and rolled onward to the region of the West. . . and of the North: and there too happened as had happened in the Southern and West.

Then when the Celestial Wheel had gone forth conquering over the whole earth to its ocean boundary, it returned to the royal city, and stood, so that one might think it fixed, in front of the judgement hall at entrance to the inner apartments of the king, the Wheel-turner, lighting up with its glory the facade of the inner apartments of the king, the sovereign of the world.

(8) And a second king. brethern, also a Wheel-turning monarch,. . . and a third. . . and a fourth. . . and a fifth. . . and a sixth. . . and a seventh king, a victorious war-lord, after many years, after many hundred years, after many thousand years, command a certain man, saying:

'If thou should'est see, sirrah, that the Celestial Wheel has sunk down, has slid from its place, bring me word.' 'Even so, sire.' replied the man.

So after many years, after many hundred years, after many thousand years, that man saw that the Celestial Wheel had sunk down, had become dislodged from its place. And so seeing he went to the king, the warlord, and told him.

Then that king did (even as Strongtyre had done). And on the seventh day after the royal hermit had gone forth the Celestial Wheel disappeared.

Then a certain man went and told the King. Then the King was grieved at the disappearance of the wheel, and afflicted with grief. But he did not go to the hermit-king to ask concerning, the Ariyan Duty of sovereign war-lord. But his own ideas, forsooth, he governed his people; and they so governed differently from what they had been. did not prosper as they used to do under former kings who had carried out the Arivan duty of a sovereign king.

Then, brethren, the ministers and courtiers, the finance officials, the guards and door keepers and they *who* lived by sacred verses came to the King and speak thus:

'Thy people, O king. whilst thou governest them by thine own ideas differently from the way to which they were used when former kings were carrying out the Arivan Duty prosper not. Now there are in thy kingdom ministers and courtiers, finance officers, guards and custodians, and they who live by sacred verses—both all of us and others—who keep the knowledge of the Ariyan duty of the sovereign king. to ! O king. do thou ask us concerning it: to thee thus asking will we declare it.'

9. Then, brethren, the king, having made the ministers and all the rest sit down together, asked them about the Ariyan duty of Sovereign war-lord. And they declared it unto him. And when he had heard them, he did provide the due watch and ward protection, but on the destitute he bestowed no wealth and because this was not done, poverty became widespread.

When poverty was thus become rife, a certain man took that which others had not given him, what people call by theft. Him they caught, and brought before the king, saying: 'This man, O king has taken that which was not given to him and that is theft'.

Thereupon the king speak thus to the man. 'Is it true sirrah, that thou hast taken what no man gave thee, hast committed what men call theft.' It is true, O king.' 'But why?'

'O king, I have nothing to keep me alive.' Then the king bestowed wealth on that man, saying: 'With this wealth sir, do thou both keep thyself alive, maintain thy parents, maintain children and wife, carry on thy business.' 'Even so, O king,' replied the man.

10. Now another man, brethren, took by theft what was not given him. Him they caught and brought before the king and told him., saying: 'this man, O king, hath taken by theft what was not given him'.

And the king (spoke and did even as he had spoken and done to the former man.)

II. Now men heard brethren, that to them who had taken by theft what was not given them, the King was giving wealth. And hearing they thought, let us then take by theft what has not been given us.

Now a certain man did so. And him they caught and charged before the king who (as before) asked him why he had stolen. 'Because, O king I cannot maintain myself. Then the king thought: If I bestow wealth on anyone so ever who has taken by theft what was not given him, there will be hereby and increase of this stealing. Let me now put final stop to this and inflict condign punishment on him, have his head cut off!

So he bade his man saying ' now look ye! bind this man's arms behind him with a strong rope and tight knot, shave his head bald, lead him around with a harsh sounding drum, from road to road, from cross ways to cross ways, take him out by the southern gate and to the south of the town, put a final stop to this, inflict on him uttermost penalty, cut of his head.'

' Even so, O king ' answered the men, and carried out his commands.

12. Now men heard, brethren, that they who took by theft what was not given them were thus put to death. And hearing they thought, let us also now have sharp swords made ready for themselves, and them from whom we take what is not given us—what they call them— let us put a final stop to them, inflict on them uttermost penalty., and their heads off.

And they got themselves sharp swords, and came forth to sack village and town and city, and to work highway robbery.

And then whom they robbed they made an end of, cutting off their heads.

13. Thus, brethren, from goods not being bestowed on the destitute poverty grieve rife; from poverty growing rife stealing increased, from the spread of stealing violence grew space, from the growth of violence the destruction of life common, from the frequency of murder both the span of life in those beings and their comeliness also (diminished).

Now among humans of latter span of life, brethren, a certain took by theft what was not given him and even as those others was accused before the king and questioned if it was true that he had stolen. 'Nay, O king,' he replied, 'they are deliberately telling lies.' 14. Thus from goods not being bestowed on the destitute, poverty grew rife... stealing... violence... murder... until lying grew common.

Again a certain man reported to the king, saying ' such and such a man, O king! has taken by theft what was not given him '— thus speaking evil of him.

15. And so, brethren, from goods not being bestowed on the destitute poverty grew rife... stealing... violence... murder... lying... evil speaking grew abundant.

16. From lying there grew adultery.

17. Thus from goods not being bestowed on the destitute, poverty... stealing... violence... murder... lying... evil speaking. . . immorality grew rife.

18. Among (them) brethren, three things grew space incest, wanton greed and perverted lust.

Then these things grew apace lack of filial piety to mother and father, lack of religious piety to holy men, lack of regard for the head of the clan.

19. There will come a time, brethren, when the descendants of those humans will have a life-span of ten years. Among humans of this life span, maidens of five years will be of a

marriageable age. Among such humans these kinds of tastes (savours) will disappear; ghee, butter, oil of tila, sugar, salt. Among such humans kudrusa grain will be the highest kind of food. Even as to-day rice and curry is the highest kind of food, so will kudrusa grain will be then. Among such humans the ten moral courses of conduct will altogether disappear, the tenimmoral courses of action will flourish excessively; there will be no word for moral among such humans, the ten moral courses of conduct will altogether disappear, the ten immoral courses of action will flourish excessively, there will be no word for moral among such humans—far less any moral agent. Among such humans, brethren, they who lack filian and religious piety, and show no respect for the Head of the clan—'tis they to whom homage and praise will be given, just as to-day homage and praise are given to the filial minded, to the pious and to them who respect the heads of their clans.

20. Among such humans, brethren, there will be no (such thoughts of reverence as are a bar to intermarriage with) mother, or mother's sister, or mother's sister-in-law, or teacher's wife, or father's sister-in-law. The world will fall into promiscuity, like goats and sheep, fowls and swine, dogs and jackals.

Among such humans, brethren keen mutual enmity will become the rule, keen ill-will, keen animosity, passionate thoughts even of killing, in a mother towards her child, in a child towards its father, in brother to brother, in brother to sister, in sister to brother. Just a sportsman feels towards the game that he sees, so will they feel.

This is probably the finest picture of what happens when moral force fails and brutal force takes its place. What the Buddha wanted was that each man should be morally so trained that he may himself become a sentinel for the kingdom of righteousness.

VIII WITHERING AWAY OF THE STATE

The Communists themselves admit that their theory of the State as a permanent dictatorship is a weakness in their political philosophy. They take shelter under the plea that the State will ultimately wither away. There are two questions, which they have to answer. When will it wither away? What will take the place of the State when it withers away? To the first question they can give no definite time. Dictatorship for a short period may be good and a welcome thing even for making Democracy safe. Why should not Dictatorship liquidate itself after it has done its work, after it has removed all the obstacles and boulders in the way of democracy and has made the path of Democracy safe. Did not Asoka set an example? He practised violence against the Kalingas. But thereafter he renounced violence completely. If our victor's to-day not only disarm their victims but also disarm themselves there would be peace all over the world.

The Communists have given no answer. At any rate no satisfactory answer to the question what would take the place of the State when it withers away, though this question is more important than the question when the State will wither away. Will it. be succeeded by Anarchy? If so the building up of the Communist State is an useless effort. If it cannot be sustained except by force and if it results in anarchy when the force holding it together is withdraws what good is the Communist State. The only thing, which could sustain it after force is withdrawn, is Religion. But to the Communists Religion is anathema. Their hatred to Religion is so deep seated that they will not even discriminate between religions which are helpful to Communism and religions which are not; The Communists have carried their hatred of

Christianity to Buddhism without waiting to examine the difference between the two. The charge against Christianity levelled by the Communists was two fold. Their first charge against Christianity was that they made people other worldliness and made them suffer poverty in this world. As can be seen from quotations from Buddhism in the earlier part of this tract such a charge cannot be levelled against Buddhism.

The second charge levelled by the Communists against Christianity cannot be levelled against Buddhism. This charge is summed up in the statement that Religion is the opium of the people. This charge is based upon the Sermon on the Mount which is to be found in the Bible. The Sermon on the Mount sublimates poverty and weakness. It promises heaven to the poor and the weak. There is no Sermon on the Mount to be found in the Buddha's teachings. His teaching is to acquire wealth. I give below his Sermon on the subject to Anathapindika one of his disciples.

Once Anathapindika came to where the Exalted One was staying. Having come he made obeisance to the Exalted One and took a seat at one side and asked 'Will the Enlightened One tell what things are welcome, pleasant, agreeable, to the householder but which are hard to gain.'

The Enlightened One having heard the question put to him said ' Of such things the first is to acquire wealth lawfully.'

'The second is to see that your relations also get their wealth lawfully.'

'The third is to live long and reach great age.' 'Of a truth, householder, for the attainment of these four things, which in the world are welcomed, pleasant agreeable but hard to gain, there are also four conditions precedent. They are the blessing of faith, the blessing of virtuous conduct, the blessing of liberality and the blessing of wisdom.

The Blessing of virtuous conduct which abstains From taking life, thieving, unchastely, lying and partaking of fermented liquor.

The blessing of liberality consists in the householder living with mind freed from the taint of avarice, generous, open-handed, delighting in gifts, a good one to be asked and devoted to the distribution of gifts.

Wherein consists the blessing of Wisdom? He know that an householder who dwells with mind overcome by greed, avarice, ill-will, sloth, drowsiness, distraction and flurry, and also about, commits wrongful deeds and neglects that which ought to be done, and by so doing deprived of happiness and honour.

Greed, avarice, ill will, sloth and drowsiness, distraction and flurry and doubt are stains of the mind. A householder who gets rid of such stains of the mind acquires great wisdom, abundant wisdom, clear vision and perfect wisdom.

Thus to acquire wealth legitimately and justly, earn by great industry, amassed by strength of the arm and gained by sweat of the brow is a great blessing. The householder makes himself happy and cheerful and preserves himself full of happiness; also makes his parents, wife, and children, servants, and labourers, friends and companions happy and cheerful, and preserves them full of happiness. The Russians do not seem to be paying any attention to Buddhism as an ultimate aid to sustain Communism when force is withdrawn.

The Russians are proud of their Communism. But they forget that the wonder of all wonders is that the Buddha established Communism so far as the Sangh was concerned without dictatorship. It may be that it was a communism on a very small scale but it was communism I without dictatorship a miracle which Lenin failed to do.

The Buddha's method was different. His method was to change the mind of man: to alter his disposition: so that whatever man does, he does it voluntarily without the use of force or compulsion. His main means to alter the disposition of men was his Dhamma and the constant preaching of his Dhamma. The Buddhas way was not to force people to do what they did not like to do although it was good for them. His way was to alter the disposition of men so that they would do voluntarily what they would not otherwise to do.

It has been claimed that the Communist Dictatorship in Russia has wonderful achievements to its credit. There can be no denial of it. That is why I say that a Russian Dictatorship would be good for all backward countries. But this is no argument for permanent Dictatorship. Humanity does not only want economic values, it also wants spiritual values to be retained. Permanent Dictatorship has paid no attention to spiritual values and does not seem to intend to. Carlyle called Political Economy a Pig Philosophy. Carlyle was of course wrong. For man needs material comforts" But the Communist Philosophy seems to be equally wrong for the aim of their philosophy seems to be fatten pigs as though men are no better than pigs. Man must grow materially as well as spiritually. Society has been aiming to lay a new foundation was summarised by the French Revolution in three words, Fraternity, Liberty and Equality. The French Revolution was welcomed because of this slogan. It failed to produce equality. We welcome the Russian Revolution because it aims to produce equality. But it cannot be too much emphasised that in producing equality society cannot afford to sacrifice fraternity or liberty. Equality will be of no value without fraternity or liberty. It seems that the three can coexist only if one follows the way of the Buddha. Communism can give one but not all.

Made in the USA
Coppell, TX
29 January 2020